ACCOMPANYING BASICS
by Joyce Grill

ISBN 0-8497-9316-5

Cover photo courtesy of Kawai American Corporation.

WP154

2

PREFACE

This book is a guide for both teachers and students. For the teacher, it presents a format for covering the basics of accompanying; for the student, it is a guide to the marvelous world of accompanying, a world so different from playing piano solos.

Through accompanying, a pianist can share the magic of making music with someone else. It can open many doors – socially and musically. Pianists who accompany and play chamber music have the opportunity to know and work with more people, and to become familiar with an even larger body of great music literature.

Teaching and learning the basics of accompanying can be done in a series of group lessons, with a chapter being covered in one or two sessions. Students of different abilities can work well together in an accompanying group. If the music being discussed is too difficult for some to play, they will still benefit from the ideas discussed, and they will have excellent exposure to listening and analyzing.

An accompanying class is a good way to get pianists to congregate with others. Knowing others are interested in playing the piano is always a good reinforcement and boost for continuing to play.

The keys to success in accompanying are the same as in solo playing:

Preparation and Practice!

This book will help with the preparation; the practice is up to you!

Joyce Grill

Joyce Grill has accompanied professionally in New York and Chicago. She is currently on the staff of the University of Wisconsin-La Crosse, teaching piano and accompanying. Mrs. Grill is active accompanying faculty recitalists as well as touring professionals.

With a special desire to train even young piano students in accompanying, she gives many clinics and workshops to piano teacher groups as well as to high school and college students.

Mrs. Grill continues to be active in the East Central Division of the Music Teachers National Association and the Wisconsin Music Teachers Association.

WP154

CHAPTER 1
WHAT ABOUT ACCOMPANYING?

Why accompany? Many teachers and students have already discovered that accompanying develops good fingering habits, a better sense of phrasing, a keener harmonic sense, and a "listening" ear. Also, the opportunities to perform as an accompanist are more numerous than those for a solo pianist. The accompanist may participate with instrumental and vocal soloists, with church and school choirs, community theater, school functions, Christmas and other sing-a-longs. The pianist can enjoy the musical and social benefits of making music with others; a joy that most other musicians experience from a very early level, but that is sometimes altogether missed by the solo pianist.

The dictionary defines the word "accompany" as "to go along or in company with." This implies an equality of sorts. However, in musical settings, many people mistakenly define "accompany" as "to follow." In some instances this is true.

"Following" usually occurs when the soloist is in full control of all the elements that go into making a musical performance. Then, if the soloist feels like stretching a phrase, holding a note longer, et cetera, the accompanist "follows." Yet, many times the accompanist is the initial "leader," having to set the tempo and mood of the piece through the piano solo opening measures. This "leading" also can occur later in the piece when the pianist has the melody while the soloist has a countermelody or obbligato.

Then there are the times when the soloist is NOT in control! Even with hours of practice, in performance the soloist may forget the things that have been rehearsed, and unless the accompanist "leads" into the tempo changes, the rubatos, the phrases, many performances would not only be unmusical, but disastrous. So, in truth, the accompanist is the "leader."

The question for the accompanist then, is "How do I know when to lead or follow?" This is where another role of the accompanist comes in. It is probably one of the most important aspects of accompanying; it is the ability to "anticipate." In fact, perhaps a better word than accompanist would be "anticipator" because this is the key to being a good accompanist.

Having thoroughly studied the score, the pianist must anticipate the tempos, rubatos, dynamics, phrasing, breathing, and yes, even be prepared for the soloist's memory lapses. The pianist must then react immediately and decide whether to lead or follow, depending on which will make the most successful, musical performance. This is why the accompanist does not play from memory. It is easier to skip, adjust, et cetera, while looking at the score of both parts.

No two performers are alike in reaction to pressure – this is one reason that makes accompanying a challenge! The more an accompanist works with a particular soloist, the better the ability to anticipate the types of things that soloist will do. In other words, accompanying requires flexibility.

Another factor an accompanist must take into account is giving proper support. The following, leading, and anticipating will be of no use if the pianist cannot give the proper dynamic levels necessary not only for a musical line, but as a foundation for the soloist to work upon. The dynamic levels vary not only from soloist to soloist, but from piece to piece by the same soloist. Thus, the physical capacities of the soloist and the instrument must be considered. Careful listening is required to make the final decision.

CHAPTER 2
WHO SHOULD ACCOMPANY?

Every piano student should have an opportunity to accompany. However, not every pianist can be an accompanist. It takes a student who likes to play all kinds of music, someone who likes to work with another person, and above all, it takes one who can accept criticism even if it is not his fault.

At the district solo and ensemble contest, a Class A pianist gave a particularly beautiful performance. She played her piece very musically, with good technique, rhythm, phrasing, and dynamics. Everyone was impressed! The same pianist later appeared as an accompanist. Everyone thought it would be a marvelous performance. The girl seated herself at the piano, placed her left foot on the soft pedal and except for some vague rumblings, was never heard from again.

Why this great change? What happened to the musicianship of the piano soloist? Where was the phrasing, the rhythm, the dynamics, the ensemble, and above all, the ability to *make music* out of the printed page? Upon questioning, the girl admitted that she had the music only one week and really did not know what to do with it. Her piano teacher said she could not help her with it and the soloist's teacher just said not to play too loud. How could she have been helped?

Students should receive the accompaniment early enough so the score can be studied (preparation) and properly practiced. If piano teachers would go to the band and choral directors and indicate that they (the teacher) would help the student accompanist IF they received the music early enough, then those last-minute situations could be avoided. Also, it would relieve that one pianist who gets ten accompaniments because he or she can "learn it in a hurry." Learn, yes; play it musically, rarely!

The piano teacher must have a good knowledge of the student's capabilities and carefully match the accompaniment with the ability. Some of the easiest-looking pieces often require more musicianship than the "harder" ones requiring more technique. The student needs ample time to prepare for musical and technical problems.

The personality of the accompanist is very important. As mentioned before, the accompanist must be able to accept criticism or "blame" when the soloist skips a part. No matter how quickly or smoothly the accompanist makes the jump, it will sound as if the accompanist made a mistake. If anyone comments, however, the accompanist must be gracious and non-commital, not saying that the soloist skipped, or even inferring that the soloist was at fault. Musicians who know the piece will be aware of what happened. The accompanist will have the satisfaction of knowing that a possible disaster was averted. Students who could not cope with this sort of stress should not accompany. So, besides the credo of **Preparation and Practice (P & P),** the other most important credo is **Save Our Soloist (SOS),** at all costs, right or wrong, trying to preserve the most musical performance possible.

Teachers should remember that if they take credit for the student's solo performances, they are just as responsible for the student's accompanying performance, especially a poor one.

CHAPTER 3
GENERAL TRAINING
FOR THE ACCOMPANIST

Accompanists need the same thorough command of the basics of piano playing as a piano soloist does, especially a strong technique. For instance, Brahms' song accompaniments have the same technical problems as his piano works. (An efficient pianist will jot some fingerings in with pencil in order to facilitate technical manuevers when the mind has to be concentrating on many things.)

The technique should enable an accompanist to play legato without using the sustaining pedal and to play softly without relying on the soft pedal. A good way to practice for evenness of touch, listening, and balance of voices is to play hymns – bringing out the bass line one time, the alto voice another, et cetera.

An accompanist must have a wide range of dynamics available, because of the variances in dynamics from one instrument to another, and from one soloist to another. One person's *forte* may be another person's *piano*. The pianist needs a full rich sound AND a soft sound that does not lose vitality and strength. A good way to develop this skill is to practice scales with one hand loud, the other soft, then doing the opposite. Scales can also be practiced with crescendos and decrescendos.

The student should know the elements of theory and keyboard harmony to enable them to recognize scale and arpeggio passages with "automatic" fingering patterns.

Major and minor scales should be practiced in parallel and contrary motion. They should also be practiced with various intervals between the hands (i.e. the left hand starting on tonic and the right hand starting on the mediant) and should not always begin and end on the keynote. It will also be beneficial to practice scales starting on notes other than tonic, since much of the accompanying literature has such passages. It is helpful to SEE scales and arpeggios in print so that the pattern recognitions will help in sight-reading, and the notes and fingerings can then be "automatic." (All of these ideas can also be applied to the solo literature.)

Then too, all accompanists must be able to hold a steady tempo and play rhythms accurately. Steadiness is very important! However, holding a steady tempo does not mean being rigid, for the accompanist must also be flexible to the needs of the soloist. Counting out loud and using a metronome while practicing, especially on exercises and scale work, can be helpful.

Because an accompanist is called upon to play all kinds and styles of music, it is vital to have a good knowledge of composers and the style of playing that is appropriate for that composer. For instance, a different style of playing would be required for a Bach piece than for a Brahms piece . . . The period a piece of music was written in determines the kind of touch, pedaling, tempo that is used. Even young students can learn to discuss style, articulation and/or dynamics of their music.

All pianists can achieve a level of competency in sight-reading with practice; sight-reading should be started as soon as the student is reading music. In the beginning it is important to select sight-reading material that is easier than the music being studied. Then, the first rule of sight-reading is to keep going, no matter what happens. To help this process, decide to play at least the first beat of every measure, no matter what happens in between. This is very important! Young beginners should never sight-read music that contains concepts they have not yet learned.

One way to practice sight-reading, even from the very beginning, is take one of the student's pieces that has been learned and cut the piece into measures. Mix the measures and see if the student can "read" them, slowly, and with correct rhythms in a steady tempo. The most important rule in sight-reading is NOT to stop to correct. You should keep going, leaving out as many notes as necessary.

Before beginning to play a piece, make certain to check the time signature and key signature. Then glance through the music to see what the basic note value is (quarter, eighth) so there will be no surprises. Look also for groups of accidentals which might indicate modulations, and for scale and arpeggio patterns.

One good way to practice sight-reading is through duets. It encourages the players to keep going. It also gives them a sense of ensemble which is so important in accompanying. To do this in lesson time, the teacher can play with the student, or students who have lessons back-to-back could share some lesson time with each other. This is also a good activity for group sessions.

As students progress with their duet reading, they should take turns being the "leader" and the "follower," putting in accelerandos or ritardandos to see if they can be the "leader' and the "follower." The "follower" should try to "anticipate" what the "leader" might do. Playing with precise attacks and releases should also receive attention.

Studying the two-piano literature can be even more helpful because of the distance between the two pianists being more similar to the distance between pianist and instrumentalist, singer, or conductor.

Duets written especially for learning the above skills are in Chapter 5.

Another aid in sight-reading is the recognition of intervals on the printed page, and the feel of them on the keyboard. A pianist needs to develop the "feel" of an octave, a fifth, the dominant-tonic sequence, and chords. A C major triad feels different than a D major triad, or an E♭ major triad. A stronger awareness of how chords feel can be made through "feeling" chords in the air. For instance, in an E major triad the third finger is slighly raised, whereas for an E♭ triad, the first and fifth fingers are slightly raised. It is also wise to practice finding certain chords at the keyboard without looking at the hands.

To take the "feel" of the keyboard one step farther, use flash cards for intervals and chords in both clefs. When first using the cards, there are four steps to be followed:

see it,
say it,
feel it,
play it.

After several times of correctly identifying the cards, progress to just see it, play it, with middle steps done mentally. To encourage practice, students can be challenged to see how many they can get right within a minute or half-minute.

Most instrumentalists (and singers) have the same instrument for practice and performance. But for the pianist, whether soloist or accompanist, he is at the mercy of whatever is available at the performance site. This is one reason the pianist must listen so very carefully and be aware of how he plays various touches, dynamic levels, articulation, et cetera. The pianist must be able to adjust these depending on the action or tone quality of different pianos (some pianos sound lighter or heavier, brighter or darker). This is especially important for the accompanist because of the responsibility to the soloist to make certain the performance is balanced and musical.

The tape recorder can be an excellent aid to the accompanist and/or soloist. The teacher should record the student playing the accompaniment. Listen to it while watching the score, discussing good passages as well as ones needing work.

Then record the piece with the soloist. Both performers should listen and follow the score, noting ensemble considerations: attacks, releases, lines together, articulation, dynamics, tone color, etc. Also, evaluate the tempos, accelerandos, ritardandos, etc.

For a solo pianist, every effort is usually made to have a good, in tune, piano. But accompanists are often told that the piano is not the best, but "since it's only an accompaniment . . ." This can be devastating, especially for a young or inexperienced accompanist. If possible, the accompanist should try to play the piano to be used. It would be helpful to have a dress rehearsal using the same instruments, and someone to listen for balance from the audience's place. Acoustics vary in different rooms, and what sounds dead on stage may actually be carrying very well out into the hall. What sounds balanced on stage may be too soft or too loud in the hall.

Other items to check out in the performance situation are the lighting, making certain that the light is not shining in the pianist's eyes when looking at the music or at the soloist, and that there is no glare – or shadow – on the music.

Before going into a performance, the pianist should be aware that nervousness is natural. Student and teacher – and the soloist – can work together on discussing ways to make good use of the "nerves." It is expected that a conscientious accompanist does not express his nervousness to the soloist. In fact, the accompanist is expected to assume the role of coach and supporter for the soloist BEFORE the performance as well as during. The accompanist can be a calming influence, reacting to the soloist's needs whether it is sensing the soloist's need to be left alone, or the need to engage in conversation, or the need to discuss certain problems in the upcoming piece. Each soloist is different, another reason the accompanist must be "flexible" and "anticipate." The amount of nervousness is often in direct proportion to the amount of preparation and practice.

Students truly interested in accompanying should attend as many recitals as possible, making note of what accompanists do. Volunteering to turn pages can "teach" many do's and don'ts. Attending recitals are a marvelous way of learning repertoire. Sightreading seems easier if one has heard the piece before.

Recordings are another way to hear repertoire. It is valuable to hear how different artists perform the same piece.

Sightreading through the repertoire with or without a soloist can be very beneficial.

The keys to success are **Preparation and Practice.**

CHAPTER 4
FURTHER PREPARATION AND PRACTICE

Many students do not develop sight-reading skills because the only music in their homes is the music they are currently studying, or books that they have already mastered. Teachers can help to improve this situation by providing their own lending library, asking the public library to establish a piano music section with the teacher's recommendations, or helping students form their own network of exchanging books. Hymns, folk songs, and nursery rhymes are often good choices. The most important goal is to get students to sight-read, but remember, the music for sight-reading should be below or at the student's current level of study.

To make scales more inviting, set up a scale competition in the studio. Assign scales at certain metronome markings to be played a certain number of octaves according to the student's abilities. Keep a chart, either in the studio or the student's notebook, showing the student's progress. Later, dynamics, articulations, etc. can be added. Or the scale work could be done in teams to create more interest and sense of ensemble.

The following duets and suggestions can be used for ensemble practice. These are just a few of the numerous interesting duet collections available. Students must work out a method of starting together. It is preferable to become sensitive to one of the player's taking a breath or giving a nod-of-the-head cue, instead of always relying upon a whispered counting cue. That would not be possible in an accompanying situation! To work out ritardandos, one player may "guide" the tempo by lifting the left hand wrist, or breathing as an upbeat to the next notes. Slow tempos, especially, will require a lot of attention for the preciseness of a steady beat. Pianists must be aware that releases are just as important as attacks (striking a note/chords precisely together). Again, work on leading, following, and anticipating. Besides the duets in the following list, duets written specifically to enhance learning skills frequently used in ensemble music are printed in the following chapter.

Excerpts from these duets are shown on the following pages.
"Sailor's Song" from **Duet Favorites** Level 1 by Jane Bastien, (Kjos WP60)
"Serenade" by Gretchaninoff from **Twice as Nice**, Volume 1, edited by Weekley & Arganbright (Kjos WP57)
"Evening Hymn" by Gurlitt from **Twice as Nice**, Volume 1, edited by Weekley & Arganbright (Kjos WP57)
"Plantation" from **Headin' South** by Eugenie R. Rocherolle, (GWM/Kjos GP326)
Pachelbel's Canon arranged by Weekley & Arganbright (Kjos WP1047)
Waltz for Two Pianos by Eugenie R. Rocherolle (GWM/Kjos GP349)
Jazz Theme and Variations by Arletta O'Hearn (Kjos WP89)

from **Duet Favorites** by Jane Bastien

Sailor's Song
Secondo

Sailor's Song
Primo

from **Twice as Nice**, Volume 1 ed. by Weekley & Arganbright

Serenade
Op. 99 No. 10

Alexander T. Gretchaninoff
edited by Weekley and Arganbright

Evening Hymn
Op. 178 No. 13
from Little Flower Pieces

Cornelius Gurlitt
edited by Weekley and Arganbright

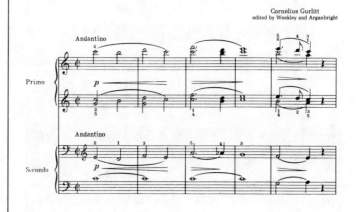

from **Headin' South** *by Rocherolle*

Plantation

from **Pachelbel's Canyon** *arr. by Weekley & Arganbright*

Pachelbel's Canon in D

from **Waltz for Two Pianos** *by Rocherolle*

Waltz for Two Pianos

from **Jazz Theme and Variations** *by O'Hearn*

JAZZ THEME & VARIATIONS
for two pianos

CHAPTER 5
SPECIALIZED TRAINING: AN OVERVIEW

Teachers and students will probably benefit most if the specialized training for accompanying is given in a group situation. Students should understand that everything that they are learning in their regular piano lessons is necessary for accompanying skills. Monthly group lessons could focus on accompanying throughout the semester or year. A particularly good time for emphasizing accompanying is in December using Christmas carols. The few weeks after Christmas are also good times to help students gain accompanying skills. There is often a letdown after Christmas, the students often have not practiced their solo assignments well, and it is a good time to start getting interest for accompanying for spring contests, festivals, or concerts.

Students usually enjoy the group situations. Playing the piano is an "alone" skill: you practice alone, you have your lesson alone, and you usually perform alone. The clarinetist or the violinist can join an orchestra or band for a group experience, but except for occasional "monster piano concerts" or "regular" duet playing, pianists play alone. Accompanying provides a social and musical interaction. It often can be a factor in keeping a student interested in playing the piano. Accompanying is also a skill that can be enjoyed throughout life, and is usually in demand whether at the professional or amateur level.

There are many different kinds of accompanying: voice, instrumental, regular and swing choirs, musicals, chamber music, and dance – ballet, tap, and modern. Each kind of accompanying has some of the same general problems, but each has problems unique to it.

Some of the general skills needed to be developed are presented in the following duets. They can be played by students of various levels by adjusting tempo markings to fit techniques (no tempo markings are given). Dynamics have not been indicated and can also be the performers' choice. The crucial part at any dynamic level is *balance*. The melody must be louder than the accompanying figures. Doubled melodies such as in *Bell Waltz* and *A Tandem Waltz* must also balance and be louder than the accompanying figures. Players should practice together just the melody and then just the accompaniment, listening carefully to match parts.

Each duet stresses one technical area found in ensemble playing, whether in duets, two-piano works, or accompanying. Each of the duets should be practiced in the following way:

- Learn both parts of the duet. After each part is learned, the student should hum, whistle, or "ta-ta" the other part while playing one part. In accompanying it is essential to "hear" the other part and thus be able to react to it.
- Play the duet with another pianist (student or teacher), deciding which person will be the leader.
- Pay particular attention to attacks and releases. The leader should breathe, just as a conductor gives an upbeat, to begin the piece.
- How to release at the end of the piece, or a section, needs to be decided. Normal choices are to hold the last notes for exactly so many beats, or the leader can cue the release with an exaggerated lifting of the wrists. The person using the pedal must also remember to release the pedal exactly with the hands.
- With these duets, partners may experiment with the pedaling. In the past it has been more common for the secondo to pedal with the harmonic changes, but today it is also accepted that the primo would pedal the melody line. In general, the pedaling partner has to accommodate both harmony and melody.

This is a duet between the primo and secondo parts. Attention must be given to playing the notes precisely together. In bars 2 and 4, and similar places, the notes in the primo right hand and the secondo left hand must sound like a part of the phrase. In the last two bars before the *D.C. al Fine,* the quarter notes must sound like a continuous line.

Bell Waltz

Joyce Grill

*Tempos and dynamics have been left to the discretion of the performer.

In accompaniments there are often measures of rests for the pianist. It is important to "hear" the other part during the rests rather than just relying on counting – it's possible that the soloist might not play exactly as written and rehearsed! When practicing without the duet partner, the pianist should "hear" the pitches of the other part while "ta-ta-ing" the rhythm aloud. When playing together, the partners should aim for long lines, making it sound as if one person was playing. Play at different tempos, especially slow, as it requires even more concentration to keep dynamics equal and lines smooth.

Popcorn

Joyce Grill

*( ) indicates a shared note.

This is a duet between the primo and secondo parts, with each part having a melodic figure and part of the accompanying figure. Be sure to practice the "oom chick chick" parts as a team, so they sound like one person is playing.

A Tandem Waltz

Joyce Grill

*Tempos and dynamics have been left to the discretion of the performer.

Count and listen very carefully so that the half note chords (starting in bar 2) come precisely together. When the ensemble is perfected, transpose to other keys! Practice with a crescendo-decrescendo spread over bars 1 and 2; then practice the reverse.

Scaling the Heights

Joyce Grill

*Tempos and dynamics have been left to the discretion of the performer.

*( ) indicates a shared note.

**Notes between [   ] may be omitted.

As a duet team, practice with a crescendo/decrescendo spread over each two-bar phrase; then practice the reverse. Remember that the urge to play faster/slower for the crescendo/decrescendo must be resisted!

Hang Glider's Club

Joyce Grill

*Tempos and dynamics have been left to the discretion of the performer.

Practice clapping the rhythm of this piece ♩ ♪ ♪ ‖: ♫ ♫ :‖ slightly stressing the downbeats. This piece is excellent preparation for the many accompaniments that have patterns switching from down beats to off-beats.

Switching Partners

Joyce Grill

*Tempos and dynamics have been left to the discretion of the performer.

The smooth melody must fit over the choppy accompaniment without sounding like the performers are counting in four. This piece should really sound as if there was one beat per bar: bar 1 is beat 1, bar 2 is beat 2, etc.

Spanish Dance

Joyce Grill

*Tempos and dynamics have been left to the discretion of the performer.

It is important to "hear" two notes against three notes. This piece not only gives pianists the opportunity to work on playing two notes over the same beat as the other pianist is playing three notes, but also the chance to practice changing from duples to triplets within the same part. Each partner needs to maintain an even, smooth line. Special attention and listening will need to be given to the measures surrounding the *rubato*.

Twos Versus Threes

Joyce Grill

*Tempos and dynamics have been left to the discretion of the performer.

This piece will help students become accustomed to switching from one rhythmic grouping to another. Using a metronome, clap the rhythms before trying to play them. The danger is to go *too* fast as more notes are added.

Clap:

Metronome: x   x   x   x

A fun way to practice is in a group situation where the teacher, or another student, claps the beat and calls out for 2's, 3's, 4's, etc. to be clapped by others.

Progressive Peter

Joyce Grill

*Tempos and dynamics have been left to the discretion of the performer.

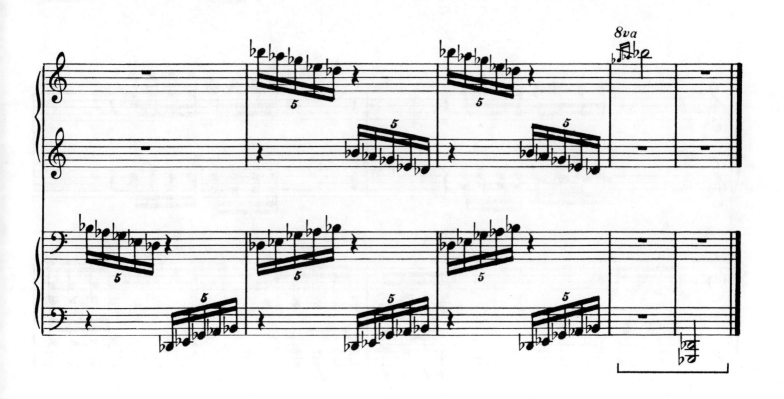

This piece requires relaxed, loose, "hinged" wrists; and it needs to be practiced very slowly at first. Speed and endurance will be impossible with a stiff wrist. As a duet, the line must pass smoothly from one part to the other, with no accents.

Play It Again, Sam

Joyce Grill

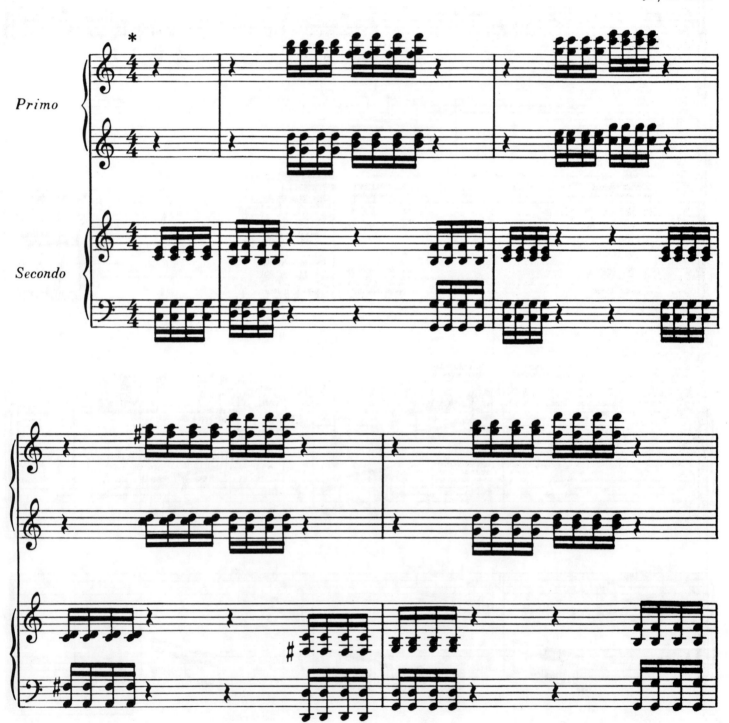

*Tempos and dynamics have been left to the discretion of the performer.

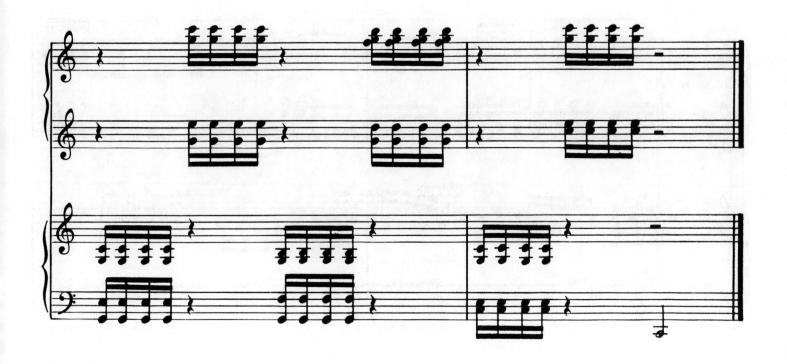

Fingering is critical for obtaining a continually smooth line (with no bumps!) with the sixteenth notes. Any extra fingerings should be written in with pencil. This piece presents a few areas specific to duet playing: the closeness of arms and fingers, and hands crossing over one another. For the crossovers it is often easier for the secondo to cross over the primo, but both ways should be tried.

Double Cross

Joyce Grill

*Tempos and dynamics have been left to the discretion of the performer.

*( ) indicates a shared note.

CHAPTER 6
THE CHORAL ACCOMPANIST

Students are most often called upon to accompany a choir of some kind, whether at school or church. The accompanist must be sensitive to the needs of a conductor and use all skills to assist and support, but never interfere.

One of the important principles in this type of accompanying is to learn to follow the conducting patterns. The group lesson is an ideal time for students to learn the basic conducting patterns. To begin each pattern, use just a slight uplift of the hand before the downbeat and take a breath at the same time.

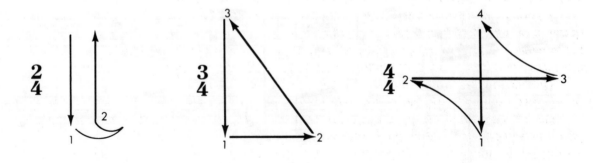

The position of the piano during rehearsals is very important. The piano should be placed so the pianist can see the conductor's beat while looking at the music.

Now have someone conduct a simple piece such as *America,* and see if the pianist can watch the conductor and play. Continue taking turns so that everyone can be an accompanist, a conductor, and a member of the chorus! Familiar songs such as *Old MacDonald* and *London Bridge* are good to practice with. (More advanced students should become familiar with *Messiah* by Handel, *The Creation* by Haydn, *Requiem Mass* by Mozart and the *Mass in G* by Schubert.) The conductor should try to include some ritardandos and accelerandos. Also practice attacks and releases. Everyone must try to do what the conductor indicates!

During a piano lesson the teacher can conduct one of the solo pieces the student is preparing, or conduct a sight-reading piece, just to give the student the feel of watching the conductor.

The accompanist must understand that the conductor is in charge, and that the accompanist must assist and give support, not interfere. In helping the student prepare for such an accompanying situation, the piano teacher can help with tempo, style, and technical problems, but the final decision on interpretation is up to the conductor.

A knowledge of major triads and arpeggios in all keys is essential in playing the warm-up exercises. The dominant-tonic progression in all keys is also important. Accompanists should learn what warm-up exercises the conductor likes to use. They should be practiced in certain rhythms, without pedal, and fairly loud. Warm-up exercises are good to practice in the group lesson on accompanying. They are valuable for theory as well as piano technique. These same type exercises are used by the solo singer as well.

Before the rehearsal the accompanist should circle rehearsal numbers in the music and locate the sections. He should know the words and have a good sense of the structure. Conductors usually go back to the beginning of phrases. (Piano students are often accustomed to going back to the beginning of a line instead of a phrase!) Add accidentals with a pencil in modulatory passages for faster, more accurate recognition.

Be sure to take a pencil with eraser to the rehearsals. When giving pitches, play from the bottom up, slowly, listening to make sure each section has the note, repeating one if necessary after they have all been played.

When playing a single line for a section of the chorus (tenors, etc.) double it at the octave in order to help the section hear it more clearly. Again, play it loud, with no pedal. IMPORTANT! The tenor part is written in the treble clef, but it is played (and sung) an octave lower.

Open score reading – playing all choral lines – requires practice just like all other skills. For learning this skill, first play the soprano and alto lines, then just the tenor and bass lines. Next read the soprano and bass lines together so the eye gets accustomed to the wide spacing. Finally, play all four parts at one time. A knowledge of keyboard harmony, especially aural, will make the sight-reading easier because you will be able to anticipate what is expected. Try and read horizontally (which is how one normally reads) as well as vertically (to get all pitches for the chorus). It is important, as always, to keep going.

When playing the choral parts in rehearsal, be sure to play the entrances and the important melodic and harmonic passages. Try to retain the bass line at all times. If one part must be omitted, leave out the soprano as they usually have the melody and learn it quickly. Never sacrifice the pulse in order to play right notes! Be careful to at least keep the harmony going on page turns. In tricky rhythmic patterns, mark the main beats with a pencil.

Mark the score with any special instructions the conductor gives the chorus. The accompanist might need to take over a rehearsal, or play for a sectional rehearsal. It is the accompanist's responsibility to know what the conductor has demanded.

In rehearsals, it is most important that the accompanist pay attention at all times. As soon as the conductor stops the group, try to anticipate where the conductor will want to start. Be ready to give the pitches, but at the same time, listen to why the conductor stopped.

As the chorus learns their parts, start playing the accompaniment, helping with parts only when necessary. Often the conductor will indicate when he wants the accompaniment played.

It is imperative that the accompanist follow the conductor, right or wrong. The accompanist has to give up the temptation to make a ritardando if the conductor does not direct it.

If the accompanist is taking the place of an orchestra during the rehearsals, he should not skip a measure to stay with the group if they come in early or late. An orchestra cannot skip measures!

Even though the piano may not be used at the final performance, the accompanist should learn the introductions and postludes. They should be played in the correct style even if it means leaving out notes. Again, a steady rhythm is essential. The long legato phrases of Bach cantata accompaniments on the piano can be very choppy unless the pianist carefully sacrifices some of the notes so the lines will flow smoothly. The piano style will affect the singers' style.

CHAPTER 7
THE ART SONG

Many states have spring music contests or festivals where solo voice is a category and the pieces are chosen from the art song repertoire. When the great composers were inspired to set the poetry of Goethe, Heine, Eichendorff and Verlaine to music, they conceived the voice and piano part at the same time, as a whole entity. Yet students who perform these songs, especially in the original language, often have no idea what the song is about and so the interpretation suffers. As the great accompanist Gerald Moore noted, the accompaniment is used to paint pictures or evoke a mood; it reflects the words. So in order to play the part effectively, the pianist must understand the poem. When asked what a song is about, a student might reply "night." But is it a summer night, a winter night, calm, windy, starry, cloudy, or what? Can you imagine what a difference it makes in the interpretation of the song just knowing what *kind* of night the poem is about?

In learning a song accompaniment, the accompanist should follow these basic steps. First, read a good translation of the poem to try and sense the mood of the work. Two books containing good translations are:

The Penguin Book of Lieder, Edited by Prawer, Penguin Books, Baltimore 1964.

The Ring of Words, Selected by Miller, Doubleday/Anchor, New York 1963.

Pianists truly interested in accompanying should also make a word for word translation. Better still, the accompanist and the singer should read the poem out loud together to be sure they both understand the poem. Often, beginning singers have no idea what the song is about, having merely learned words with notes while worrying more about their technique.

Secondly, play the melody alone, noting how the melody and rhythm fit the words. Next, play through the accompaniment, slowly, with a steady tempo, making note of any technically difficult passages. Determine what part the accompaniment plays in the interpretation of the poetry. Then decide what kind of tone color and articulation is appropriate. When the accompaniment is learned up to tempo and is under control, the pianist should sing, hum, or whistle the melody while playing the accompaniment in order to see how the two parts fit together. Breath marks should be marked in the score with a pencil (an accompanist's best tool!). Try to anticipate the dynamics or any rubato the soloist might use. The accompanist must also study the score to anticipate where it might be necessary to stretch a phrase, or speed up. Knowledge of the composer and the style of that time should be important factors in interpreting the song.

Since singers have different vocal ranges, songs are published in several different keys. The pianist may eventually play the same song in different keys if playing for several singers. Patterns that have been carefully worked out in one key often feel awkward in another. Any change in fingering patterns should be written in. Accidentals and modulations should be carefully noted. The "new" key can give the piece a different sound. Such an example is *Die Forelle* by Schubert. In the original key of E♭, the accompaniment ripples gracefully along. However, in the lower key of D♭, if great care is not taken, the graceful trout becomes a clumsy carp!

Before rehearsing, both performers should have the music well prepared and studied. The rehearsal is the time for working on the interpretation, establishing tempo, checking balance, watching phrasing and rubato, exchanging views. It is not a question of who is right or wrong, but what is musically correct or incorrect. After all, the end result is to have a musical performance. Both performers need to be a little flexible in their views.

A good opportunity to study the art of accompanying songs can be taken through group sessions with piano students. Each pianist could learn one or two song accompaniments for presentation to the class. Pianists could be singers as well, or ideally, a singer familiar with the songs could be invited to participate. If the music is too difficult for the pianists, it is still beneficial to listen to recordings as the students follow the score and discuss what problems are in the music and how they could be worked out.

One of the easiest ways to achieve a mood change is to increase or decrease the tempo. However, many songs require a steady tempo throughout. Concentrate on dynamics, articulation, or stressing different notes to help achieve the change. Examples are Schubert's *Abschied, Was ist Sylvia,* and *Gretchen am Spinnrade.*

A composer will often double the melody in the piano part. Great care must be taken with the balance in these cases. The balance in a particular song will often depend on whether the singer is a man or woman. In *Caro mio ben* by Giordani and *Widmung* by Franz, the voice line is doubled in the treble of the piano part. Therefore, the balance is more difficult with a female singer since the doubling occurs in the same octave. For instance, in Brahms' *Sandmannchen,* the accompaniment is basically in the treble clef with the melody doubled between the piano and the female voice. It will sound very different with the octave lower male voice.

In the published piano version of *O Mio Babbino Cara* from Puccini's opera, *Gianni Schicci,* the female voice part is doubled in octaves. In this case more weight should be given to the upper octave and less on the lower note which is in the singer's range. In the tenor aria *E luceven le stelle* from Puccini's opera, *Tosca,* the pianist needs to give more weight on the upper octaves because it is out of the tenor's range.

Sometimes the piano has the melody and the voice is like an obbligato. In *Morgen* by Richard Strauss, the piano plays almost the whole song as the introduction, setting a mood which the singer comments on as the piano plays it again.

Introductions not only set the tempo but establish the mood, whereas the postludes are the final comment on the song. Both should be considered as piano solos. They should also be studied to see how they relate to the song as a whole. Good examples can be found in Schubert's *Wanderer's Nachtlied, Der Wanderer, Der Neugierige;* Wolf's *Auf ein altes Bild, Ich hab in Penna einen Liebsten;* and Schumann's *Frauenlieben und leben.*

If the singer begins the piece, or starts exactly with the accompaniment, practice how to start: either with the pianist giving a single pitch or a rolled chord. Play whatever is chosen with enough tone for the singer to hear it; do not be apologetic. The pianist must watch the singer breathe so both musicians are thinking in tempo at the same time. The singer will give the cue to start by taking a breath in the tempo of the song. Examples of the pianist and singer starting together are in Schubert's *Haidenroslein,* Franz's *Widmung,* Brahms' *Der Schmied* and *Am Sonntag.* Examples of the singer starting first are in Brahms' *Der Gang zum Liebchen* and Schumann's *Die Rose, die Lilie, die Taube.*

Balance danger spots occur when the singer's voice part goes from high to low. Such a spot occurs in *Zueignung* by Strauss in measures 24-25.

When accompanying a singer, play ON the vowel sound, do not try to come with the consonant. This is especially important if the soloist is singing in a foreign language. With rolled chords, the top note should coincide with the singer's attack of the melody note.

A good song for analyzing is Brahms' *Die Mainacht,* which is shown on page 36. The two-bar introduction sets the mood and continues after the singer enters. At bar 15 there is a key, register, and mood change! The piano part must build into forte at bar 20, being aware of the singer's sudden drop in range in bar 22.

At bar 27 a very long sustained phrase begins for the singer. The pianist must be very alert here and anticipate the singer's needs. It will often be necessary to slightly increase the tempo in order for singers, especially young ones, to sing it in one breath. A crescendo is indicated but should not be too big too soon, depending on what the singer does on the whole note in bar 29. The lovely interlude brings back the original mood.

In bar 33 the piano part has more motion than at the beginning, but it still must convey a calm mood. Bar 39 begins another long phrase for the singer. Again, a crescendo in bar 44 must be timed so that the singer's entrance in bar 45 will not be overpowered. As the singer's line descends with a dimuendo the balance is especially critical. The piano concludes with a lovely calm postlude with a rising figure in the right hand against a descending inner line in the bass.

Other points to consider in analyzing are the changes in playing that might have to be made depending on whether a man or woman is singing the piece.

Die Mainacht

(The May Night)

op. 43 no. 2

Johannes Brahms

Sehr langsam und ausdrucksvoll

Wann der sil - ber - ne

Mond durch die Ge - sträu - che blinkt, und sein schlummern-des

Licht ü - ber den Ra - sen streut, und die Nach - ti - gall flö - tet,

37

WP154

und die ein- sa- me Thrä - - - - - -ne rinnt.

Wann, o lä - chelndes Bild, wel - ches wie Mor - gen - roth

durch die See - le mir strahlt, find' ich auf Er- den dich?

CHAPTER 8
ORCHESTRAL REDUCTIONS

The pianist must often cope with orchestral reductions when an instrumentalist is playing a concerto or a vocalist is singing an operatic aria. The reductions were usually meant for study rather than performance purposes, thus they are literal versions of the orchestral score, and are not necessarily pianistic. When making cuts or editing the reduction it is best to consult a full score when possible, and listen to a recording. It is important to know what instruments are used throughout the piece so they can be imitated in the appropriate places.

When a full orchestral sound is desired the piano part can be enriched by enlarging chords or by doubling the bass. Sometimes a redistribution of parts can facilitate the accompaniment.

Piano reductions frequently have a lot of repeated notes, which the orchestral string sections can play easily. On the piano, however, they are sometimes best rearranged in an Alberti pattern. The following examples show what is often found in a reduction, and one way to modify it.

Orchestral reduction

Playing version

String instrumentalists can play parallel thirds passages much easier than a pianist. In such passages it is quite acceptable to leave out the lower third entirely, or to retain it only on the strong beats.

Orchestral reduction

Playing version

Repeated octaves often occur in reduced orchestral passages. On the piano, these may be played as broken octaves. If octaves are written to be doubled in both hands, they may be reduced to three octave combinations divided between the hands. The simplification depends on the tempo of the passage, and the leaps involved.

Concerto No. 1 for Horn in F by Mozart reduction

Playing version

Tremulo parts, especially long ones, should be played with a measured beat to help keep the tempo steady. If needed, they should be rearranged so they fit comfortably under hand, giving the pianist a more relaxed position.

Violin Concerto op. 61 by Saint-Saens. Tremulos to be played in a measured beat.

The following orchestral example could be cut in several ways. A small hand could eliminate the octaves in the bass and play just the lower note. The right hand should go to an eight note pattern using either the first three notes as a chord (D F♯ D) or just playing a sixth (F♯ D). Since it is a tutti (meaning full orchestra) passage, the main thing is to give a full orchestral sound that is steady and that creates excitement.

Concerto No. 26 for Piano by Mozart.

Style is an important consideration in rearranging the accompaniment. An appropriate accompaniment pattern can often be made by comparing the treatment of the theme in the solo part to the theme in the orchestra, especially in classic concertos.

When it is necessary to cut the orchestral exposition in a classic concerto, the accompanist should be sure to play at least the A theme and then make a cut to four or eight measures before the soloist enters, trying to make as smooth a change as possible. It is important to include the theme (as opposed to starting just four or eight bars before the soloist enters); it gives the soloist and the audience a better feeling of the mood and tempo of the piece. Whenever making cuts, do not eliminate important cues.

Each pianist will cut the same score differently, depending on the individual's capabilities. The goal is to play a musical performance that will give the soloist the feel of the full orchestra.

To demonstrate some possible ways of cutting an orchestral reduction, portions of Alexander Goedicke's *Concert Etude for Trumpet* are shown the way it is available in print (published by G. Schirmer), along with the same version with an accompanist's markings. Remember that the types of cuts to be used depend on the pianist's ability.

In bar 1, the opening chord spacing is dangerous. Simplify it to insure a firm, precise beginning to the piece. The pianist should be aware that the opening trumpet melody is repeated throughout the piece in both trumpet and piano parts. It is always important to bring it out, such as in bar 4.

Excerpts from *Concert Etude for Trumpet* op. 49 by Alexander Goedicke

Bar 7 is a difficult spot for the trumpet player. Unless the pianist can hold the left hand sixteenth notes even, they should be cut to just quarter notes, or eighths. It is also important to make the crescendo with the trumpet part.

In bars 10 and 11 the octaves in the left hand can be eliminated to either the upper or lower line to insure a good crescendo. If there are still ensemble problems, the pianist could play just octaves on the beat (marked with an arrow).

Bar 10
Original, edited with pencil

In bars 15-18 the right hand arpeggios can be played as blocked chords on the beat, with the left hand as written. This is a solo passage for the piano as well as being a transition passage which must diminuendo nicely into the new theme.

Bar 15
Original

May be played:

The section starting in bar 19 is a lovely duet between the trumpet and piano, and should be brought out. In bars 21 and 22, if necessary, play just the top line of the right hand and a single line in the left hand. The same applies in bars 25-26.

Bar 19
Original, edited with pencil

Cuts should be marked in pencil. Remember, it is better to mark everything rather than expect-ing the brain to remember under the pressures of performance!

Other concertos that would be good to analyze are two by Mozart: *Piano Concerto No. 26* (D Major) K.537 and the *Horn Concerto No. 3* K.477.

For practice in score cutting, redistribution, rearranging, etc. consider Gliere's *Concerto for Horn & Orchestra* op. 91; Saint Saens' *Morceau de Concert* op. 94; Tchaikovsky's *Violin Concerto in D*; and the complete Goedicke *Concert Etude for Trumpet.*

CHAPTER 9
INSTRUMENTAL ACCOMPANYING & CHAMBER MUSIC

The festivals and contests that are popular with singers also get attention from instrumentalists – sometimes even more so. Besides the opportunities to perform in these situations, there are numerous occasions for pianists to play with brothers, sisters, and/or parents who play other instruments.

The meaning of an instrumental piece is not as obvious as that of a song where the words can help make the composer's intentions clear! When playing music with other instrumentalists, all the pianist's musical skills are needed to interpret the piece.

To gain a good ensemble with an instrumentalist the pianist needs to learn how each instrument "speaks." Some instruments take longer to sound than others. Beyond this factor, the pianist must anticipate what the soloist is going to do by watching the soloist breathe. For the attacks and releases to be exactly together it will require more than just an inner sense of precision and timing.

Each instrument, just like the voice, has ranges which can cause balance problems. Generally speaking, the lower pitched instruments require a greater clarity of articulation in the piano part, less emphasis on the bass part and less pedal than usual.

The higher instruments can generally stand more in the piano bass line, except in their lower registers. Careful listening, always, is the key – especially when the piano is playing in the same register as the instrument.

The pianist must remember that the instrument will not always be playing the exact pitches as shown on the music. This is because some instruments are *transposing* instruments. When some instrumentalists play the note "C," they sound a different pitch. The pianist should also know the intervallic difference in notation and sound. Other instruments, such as the viola and sometimes the trombone and cello, use a clef pianist's are not familiar with – the alto clef (the third line is middle C):   See the chart on the next page.

Pianists must learn what note the instrumentalist will want the pianist to play for tuning. Although most wind players will tune to B♭ or A, that can change from piece to piece. Pianists should write in (with pencil!) the tuning note. String players tune to an A, and oftentimes want a D minor triad after they have tuned the A.

In all of the music to be performed with an instrumentalist, both performers must decide together what types of articulations to use, how to ornament specified notes, what dynamics to use, and they must work together to get precise attacks and releases. The pianist must produce exactly the same length of staccato as the instrumentalist, and imitate the bowing and tonguing articulations.

Two markings that are specifically for string instruments are those used to indicate bow directions. V indicates up an bow, and ⊓ indicates a down bow.

When playing with an instrumentalist the pianist will encounter one of two different piano parts: a sonata or an accompaniment. When the piece is a sonata, both performers are considered equal (even though the piano part is often more difficult than the solo part). Sonatas are chamber music; the piano part is not an accompaniment. The pianist should take the bow at the end of the piece at the same time as the soloist, and should be listed as pianist, not accompanist, on such a program.

Many of the accompaniments (including orchestral reductions) are not very interesting to practice. They often have few technical difficulties and musical challenges for the pianist. However, the accompanist must be careful not to become too complacent; the pianist must be ever alert, anticipating problem spots in the soloist's part, and giving life to the performance.

In preparing either a sonata or an accompaniment the pianist must also know the soloist's part. This may be done by playing or singing the soloist's part first, the humming or whistling the solo part with the piano part! Even if you are unable to sing or hum the exact pitches, it will help to *attempt* a melodic line in the correct rhythm. When the pianist is able to do this, a better understanding of the ensemble is developed.

For elementary and intermediate pianists interested in playing with violinists at the same level, *Accompanying the Violin* by Katherine D. Johnson (Neil A. Kjos Music Company, WP85) provides music along with tips for learning. There is also a cassette tape available with all the music played in three ways: violin alone, piano alone, and both instruments playing together.

Transposing and Non-Transposing Instruments

Transposing	Written Note	Sounds
Bb Clarinet Bb Bass Clarinet Bb Tenor Saxophone Bb Cornet/Trumpet Bb Baritone T.C.		
Eb Alto Clarinet Eb Alto Saxophone Eb Baritone Saxophone Eb Alto Horn		
(F) French Horn (F) English Horn		

Non-Transposing	Written Note	Sounds
Flute Oboe Violin		
Viola (alto clef)		
Bassoon Trombone Baritone B.C. Tuba Cello		
Double Bass		

CHAPTER 10
THE DANCE ACCOMPANIST & THE MUSICAL

Another challenging field for accompanists is the field of dance, whether it be classical, ballet, or modern. The preparation involves learning the vocabulary particular to each, the names of dance steps and movements, and the procedures observed in a dance studio.

The ballet class is usually structured in musical phrases which are square, while the modern dance class frequently requires $\frac{5}{4}$ and $\frac{7}{4}$ meters, and constantly changing meters.

The accompanist must be sensitive to the dance movements, reflecting their style. This requires a quick music imagination! The pianist must support, not distract, the dancer. Although the accompanist may first play from a score (such as *Dance Music*) by William Peterson, WP90, Neil A. Kjos Music Company), it is important to be able to play from memory, or to improvise, in order to watch the dancers. An excellent book for thorough help is *Handbook for the Ballet Accompanist* by Gerald R. Lishka, Indiana University Press, Bloomington and London.

In high school, college, and community theaters, the pianist is called on to accompany the musical. This incorporates several features already covered in other sections of this book: following the conductor, playing vocal parts, and accompanying dances. The score often requires cutting to make it practical.

The accompaniment style is different from most of the other music discussed in this book. Accompanying a musical usually requires a lot of chording; a knowledge of I IV V I progressions in all keys is very helpful. Above all, the accompanist must be with the conductor!

For rehearsals of a musical, a reduced score including the voice parts (which are usually doubled in the piano) is used:

When performing with an orchestra, the pianist usually has just the score for piano (chording) with orchestral cues given, but no vocal score included. The score is usually in manuscript.

CHAPTER 11
STAGE PRESENCE

An audience's first impression of a performer is a visual one and yet this aspect is rarely discussed between soloists and pianists. But how important it is! When a particular symphony orchestra changed from being clothed in the traditional black to a lovely burgundy, no mention was made of this to the visiting guest soloist who appeared for the performance dressed in a beautiful red dress. It was a visual disaster! The audience gasped out loud and it was not until the second movement before the audience realized how well – or even if – the soloist was playing.

Accompanists should usually dress simply. Black or another dark color is preferable. Whether it's to be a long or short skirt, tuxedo or suit, depends on the occasion, but it does need to be discussed. Females, especially, should practice in the shoes that they will wear for the performance. Heels on dress shoes are often a different height than those for everyday rehearsals, affecting the foot action. Squeaks can also be a by-product of high heels.

Clothes are only one part of the visual presentation. How the performer walks on stage is also important. Pianists should practice walking to the piano and being seated, taking care to adjust the bench or music rack as needed. This can usually be done as the soloist is tuning (except for singers of course). The soloist and pianist need to decide in advance who will take a bow before playing. For sonatas and chamber music, all performers should take the bow together. A cue for when the bows will be taken should be given by one of the musicians. (The pianist always follows the other musicians[s] on and off stage.)

All of these details can be practiced in group classes. Pianists can take turns walking on stage, taking a bow if appropriate, sitting down and making the necessary adjustments, giving the tuning pitch, checking to see that the soloist is ready to begin, playing the "first" chord, and then "ending" a piece by just playing a chord, lifting the hands off the keyboard before standing up, then taking a bow as others clap. It is wise to practice sitting down on a bench at the wrong height and the music rack too far or too close, to give the pianist the experience of making the changes on stage.

CHAPTER 12
GENERAL TIPS FOR
THE PIANIST

Many of these suggestions apply to the solo pianist as well as the accompanist.

A performer's best ally through all rehearsals with the other musician, and through independent practice sessions, is a pencil! Mark the fingerings, wrong notes, write CALM to help you through a hard passage, draw eyeglasses to help you remember to watch for something, draw arrows to important items, and learn to react to what you have written in. In performance, always use the music which you have used during rehearsals because of the important fingerings and other markings.

Especially in a small performance hall, if you are given the choice between a 7' and a 9' grand, all things being equal, choose the 7' for accompanying purposes. Otherwise the audience may think the soloist is only pantomiming. Also, have a small block of wood handy to take the place of the short stick on a grand piano. This allows you to open the piano lid a little way so you get a clean sound, but not too much sound. The need for this will vary. It can be used for spinets and uprights, also. A block of wood as illustrated gives a choice of three different heights.

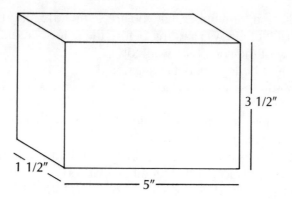

Some nervousness is to be expected. The trick is to turn the extra adrenalin into an advantage. It can make fast passages easier, provided you do not let yourself play them faster than rehearsed. It is the accompanist's responsibility to be a calming influence on the soloist. By helping the soloist remain calm, the pianist also will benefit. Taking deep breaths is a good way to help stifle the jitters. If the musicians use the time backstage to establish certain tempos before going on stage, that can help focus energy.

- To accurately set the tempo, think through a phrase in the piece before beginning. If there is a long phrase that has to be played without a breath, it may have to be the determining factor in setting the tempo of the whole piece.
- If you have to start a piece on a beat other than the downbeat, mentally give a preparatory beat as a conductor would. This will help lead you into taking a breath in the same tempo, and will be a good guide for the soloist.
- Play the printed score accurately: dynamics, ritardandos, dimunendos, rests, accents, full note values, etc.
- If you have an introduction, remember that you are setting the mood.
- Do not get into the habit of always ritarding before the soloist enters, or at the end of the piece. Always first consider what the composer wanted!
- Phrasing and rubato must be logical, not exaggerated.
- Play introductions, postludes, and interludes as if they were solos, but within the realm of the style of the music.
- Watch the soloist to achieve a better ensemble. His breathing can be a clue to tempos, rubatos, and dynamics and it can help the accompanist anticipate.
- Consider attacks and releases even more important than in the solo literature.
- Listen very carefully for balance, and remember that too soft can be as bad as too loud. For attaining an exact balance, a third person should come to listen.

- When crossing hands, mark whether over or under is more convenient. Do not rely upon the brain to remember all the details – use the pencil!

Violin Sonata by Franck

- Consider redistributing notes between hands in difficult passages. Then use the pencil to mark the changes.

Phydile by DuParc

Cello Sonata by Mendelssohn

- Accompanists rarely play from memory, but they must know the piece thoroughly in order to jump backwards or forwards should the soloist have a memory slip.
- At the end of a movement or piece, do not break the mood by withdrawing your hands from the keyboard until the soloist has definitely cut off. Then release hands and pedal together.
- If the instrumentalist has to take time between movements, be prepared to sit quietly and wait until he is ready.
- In rehearsals, practice what the cues will be for starting. With a singer it could be when he looks straight out into the hall (after having been glancing down). An instrumentalist usually gives a glance to the pianist as soon as he has stopped tuning.
- Simple accompaniments require a strong concentration on tone quality and balance. Technical songs need good fingering patterns written in.
- Know where the expected breaths will occur and be prepared to stretch or speed up slightly to accommodate. The soloist may take things a bit differently under the pressure of performance. If he needs to breathe in an unexpected place, the accompanist will need to "stretch" in the same place so they will be together.
- Use a tape recorder to tape just the accompaniment. Listen to it while watching the score, and make appropriate notes. Then record the piece with the soloist. Both performers should listen and follow the score, noting ensemble problems: attacks, releases, duet lines, articulation, dynamics, tone color, etc. Tape recorders are not always an accurate judge for balance, but they can give a basic idea.

CHAPTER 13
THE NEGLECTED ART: PAGE TURNING

The soloist and accompanist have practiced many hours alone, and together, to prepare for a free-from-worry performance. Let's consider the scene where at the last minute, the accompanist decides to use a page turner. The page turner does read music, but has had no preparation for when or how to turn. What should have been a fine performance is marked by great tension as the accompanist finds the pages are turned too late, too early, too loud, and sometimes – the whole book goes tumbling to the floor!

A good page turner is a treasure and should be cultivated and cherished. To do a good job, the page turner needs preparation and practice, too. The accompanist and page turner should talk through the music beforehand, marking things to help the turner. Any tricky page turns should be pointed out. Repeats should be marked well – especially if they are not going to be taken, or if it means turning back a page. If first endings are not going to be taken, they should be crossed out (in pencil). Cuts should also be marked well, as should Da Capos and Del Signos. The pianist should make certain that loose pages are taped and that the pages turn easily; the music should lie as flat as possible.

Decide who will turn between movements and write it on the page! If there are several measures of rests before the page turn making it possible for the pianist to turn, decide who will turn, and write it down. Some pianists feel more comfortable having the turner make all the turns, while others prefer to do easy ones themselves.

Cello Sonata in d minor op. 40 by Shostakovitch

The page turner should be at several rehearsals if possible, but definitely at the dress rehearsal. The turner usually sits to the pianist's left side on a flat bottom chair if possible, to allow the page turner to stand quietly and effortlessly. He should reach across with the left hand and "finger" the top right hand corner of the music, making sure to have only one page. It should be decided ahead of time if the pianist will nod on the turns, or if the turner should use his own judgement (this means that the pianist has a great deal of confidence in the turner!). The turner must learn to turn when the pianist nods even if there are several measures left. If it is an especially critical part the pianist may want to write "Turn here" in the score.

Cello Sonata in d minor op. 40 by Shostakovitch

Some general musical guidelines for page turners are:
- If possible, do not stand up during fermatas.
- Try not to disturb the mood. For instance, in a soft or slow passage, turn quietly and not too quickly.
- Do not let yourself become agitated by fast passages – keep counting as diligently as if you were playing.
- Do not become "lost" in the music and forget to turn.
- Do not nod, sway, or tap your hand or foot in time to the music.
- If the pages will not stay open (drafty stages are common), the turner should stand quietly and hold them open as long as necessary.

Beyond the musical considerations of a page turner, attention should also be given to what to wear. A dark suit or dress (long or short) is more appropriate than brightly colored clothing. A page turner's attire should not attract attention. Females should avoid dangling necklaces, floppy sleeves, and unrestrained long hair – all of these have the danger of obscuring the vision, or colliding with the hands of the pianist. For the same reason, a man's tie should be tacked down if a jacket does not do the job of holding the tie in. Heavy colognes, perfumes, and hairsprays should also be avoided since they can sometimes be distracting. This is true for the accompanist also.

When the performers walk on stage, the page turner follows all of the performers. Whether he carries the music and puts it on the music rack is a decision the pianist must make. The page turner should remain seated as the performers take the bows afterwards, then take the music off the piano and follow the performers off.

At all times the page turner must act and look calm, relaxed, and inconspicuous, not taking any attention away from the performers.